WORK

MW00885880

FOR

JAY SHETTY'S

THINK LIKE A

MONK

Train Your Mind for Peace and Purpose Every Day

by Intensive Life Publishing

TABLE OF CONTENTS

NOTE TO READERS

We are incredibly grateful to the author, Jay Shetty, and his publisher for giving to the world a life-changing book titled "Think Like a Monk."

This workbook is an unofficial companion for Jay Shetty's #1 Best Seller book "Think Like a Monk: Train Your Mind for Peace and Purpose Every Day." Our team of professionals carefully extracted 39 exercises from the book so that you can easily understand and incorporate them into your day-to-day life, like many others will or are already doing.

Recommendation: We strongly encourage you to incorporate these exercises into your day-to-day life so that you can significantly improve your life and consequently have a positive impact on the lives of the people around you. If you incorporate just 5 or 6 of these exercises into your life, you will indeed witness a significant change. Can you imagine how great and significant these changes will be if you incorporate 10, 20, or more? Now imagine how significant the impact could be if you go the extra mile and incorporate all of them! Can you imagine the impact you will create on the people around you and your family?

You can even go further in your thinking. Do you know that you can change other people's lives for the better through the knowledge acquired from Jay Shetty's book and this workbook? You can join thousands of people that are committed to helping others by sharing this workbook and Jay Shetty's book as a gift to those you care about; alternatively, you can share the links. Now, think about what could happen to the world if others do the same thing as you do. Remember, we are creating a better world together.

Recommendation: If you want to accelerate your growth and haven't purchased the original Jay Shetty's "Think Like a Monk" book, we encourage you to do so by visiting the link or scanning the QR code on the next page. It will give you a deeper understanding of the exercises in this companion workbook. For further general enquiries or recommendations for improvement, you can reach us at publishing@intensivelife.com.

Once again, we are sincerely grateful to the author, Jay Shetty, and his publisher for this life-transforming and valuable material. Let's spread the word about these books to the world and change more lives for the better.

If you like our effort and this companion workbook, kindly give us a review on the workbook's Amazon page.

"Think Like a Monk." A book written by Jay Shetty:

https://link.intensivelife.com/TLAM

Start your path to self-discovery.

"This testament to self-love, with an endearing coming-out story at the center, will delight readers."

Publishers Weekly on *Untamed* by Glennon Doyle

#1 *NEW YORK TIMES* BESTSELLER, over one million copies sold!

As a way of saying **THANK YOU**, we are offering a **FREE** copy of ***Summary of Untamed***. You can also be part of our Readers Circle! Visit the link or scan the QR code below:

https://link.intensivelife.com/free

Go ahead, make that first step towards discovering your authentic self.

SUMMARY OF THINK LIKE A MONK

Reading *"Think like a Monk"* by Jay Shetty is like standing on a hilltop during dawn, while the rest of the world is still asleep. It is an eye-opener.

The book is very fitting for times like these; when around the world, people are so dissatisfied or preoccupied with chasing "happiness". Shetty's goal is to show readers how to train their minds and find inner peace and purpose in their everyday life.

Scientifically speaking, monks are happier than the rest of us. Scientists who have studied monks' brain activity say that monks are calmer and happier than other people. Not all of us can join the monastic life to be happy, but we can adapt to the "monk mindset".

The book contains a combination of ancient wisdom and modern ideas that can help individuals apply the monk mentality to their daily life. It is a guide for attaining purpose and peace in life by overcoming the obstacles of negativity, fear, and ego with the help of positivity, gratitude, meditation, and service.

It can be challenging to apply these principles, so we have created a workbook that will help you incorporate the monk mindset into your daily life.

THE MONK MINDSET

The monk mindset focuses on forgiveness, energy, intentions, living with purpose, and other practices and beliefs that have been around for centuries. Monks' wisdom is supported by science and does not limit itself to meditation.

Although meditation and mindfulness are beneficial, the path to inner peace comes from gratitude and service. You will understand this better when you adopt and practice the three stages of building the monk mindset.

These stages were developed several centuries ago but are also prominent today. You don't have to force yourself into regular meditation to benefit from this workbook, although, it will make the process easier.

This workbook will force you to reflect on your beliefs, values, and intentions. It will discuss how we see ourselves, make decisions, and tackle problems.

The primary goal of this workbook is to help you connect with the timeless wisdom of monks, along with other ancient teachings that rely on the same foundations. We are sure that at the end of the workbook, you will have gained more self-awareness.

THE MONK AND THE MONKEY MIND

The monkey mind is very fluctuating and indecisive. Most of the time, it struggles with procrastination and over thinking. Our minds can either elevate or pull us down. Right now, your mind might be monkeying around. Instead, it would be best if you find stillness, calm, and peace.

This can be attained by shifting to the monk mindset, finding the root cause of what you want, and making an actionable plan to achieve it.

The monk mindset focuses on lifting you out of confusion, over thinking, and distractions. This will help you in finding clarity, meaning, and direction. You can shift from the monkey mind to the monk mind by following the exercises in this workbook.

The result of monk thinking is a life that is free of ego, envy, lust, anger, bitterness, and baggage. These negative thoughts will be transformed into calm, stillness, peace, and purpose.

GOAL OF THE WORKBOOK

The aim of this workbook is to help you train your mind for peace and purpose with the help of a few life-changing exercises. We are all searching for inner peace and purpose here on earth. This workbook is going to act like a guiding light on your path.

The ultimate purpose of life cannot be to hunt, sleep, and defend. We are here for more - gratitude, service, and love. Ever wonder what your purpose is? If not, take a step back and think about it.

You are on a journey of self-exploration; this workbook holds one primary goal, and this is to help you find the purpose you are seeking for. Get ready for this journey of self-discovery.

The exercises in the workbook are designed to create healthy and long-lasting habits that will get you back in tune with your purpose and goals. The repetition and consistency of these exercises are vital. This might be difficult initially but pay attention to how much you gain from each exercise.

USING THIS WORKBOOK

This workbook is divided into three parts. Commit to each exercise and complete it with utmost sincerity for the best outcome.

- Focus on one exercise at a time.
- Follow the workbook in the same order: part 1, part 2, and part 3.
- Do not skip exercises. If you do this, the workbook will not be effective.
- Take your time to finish an exercise but also try to exercise regularly.

Remember, this isn't a process of a day or a week. It is an exercise that will take time, EMBRACE IT! Learn to enjoy the journey and it will be a lot easier for you to adapt to this idea. We have added a section called "notes" where you can write down what you are thinking or feeling before and after completing the exercise.

LET GO. GROW. GIVE

The first part is to **let go**. Strip yourself from the external influences, internal obstacles, negativity, and fear that hold you back. This is like a cleansing act that will make space for growth.

The second part is about **growth**. It focuses on reshaping and constructing your life in a way that helps you make better decisions with clear intentions, purpose, routine, and confidence.

The final and the most important part is to **give**, look at the world beyond yourself, expand and share your sense of gratitude, and deepen your relationships. By sharing your gifts and love with others, you can discover the true joy and surprising benefits of giving.

JUST BREATHE

Before you start with the first exercise, it is important to realize that the one thing that stays with you from the moment you are born to the moment you die is your breath. You can find power in controlling your breath.

You have probably noticed that your breath changes whenever you are happy, cry or get stressed. Your breath indicates changes in your emotions. From today onwards, try to consciously monitor your breathing.

The aim of the breathing exercises is to manage your breath so that you can navigate every situation in your life and fulfill your purpose.

PART 1: LET GO

In this part of the workbook, you will identify who you are, remove the negativity from within, understand your fears and obstacles, remove yourself from external influences, and use this new understanding to focus on your intentions. By doing this, you will allow yourself the space to grow.

EXERCISE 1: IDENTITY

Often, your identity has so many layers that you lose sight of the real you. The goal of this exercise is to understand things and people that shape you, and the distractions that stop you from achieving your purpose and goals.

In life, we have a lot of forces that shape us. These can differ from person to person and experience to experience. Shaping forces can include family, money, friends, education, skills, and others. Some of these forces, such as toxic relationships, loss of loved ones, fear, negative people, and unhealthy habits can also distract us.

You will start this journey just the way monks do, by clearing away distractions.

Make a list of forces that shape you or distract you:

SHAPE   **DISTRACT**

Now, evaluate these aspects of your life and consider if they align with who you really want to be or how you want to live. Ask yourself questions: Am I spending enough time with my family? Am I earning as much as I want? Am I satisfied with the education and skills that I possess?

Write here:

The foundation of identifying your true self lies in removing distractions that prevent you from focusing on what matters the most - finding meaning in life by learning and understanding your physical and mental desires.

NOTES

EXERCISE 2: ORIGIN OF YOUR VALUES

Generally speaking, people do not enjoy being alone with their thoughts. We tend to avoid silence, try to fill our heads with mindless noise, and keep moving. In this process we forget the importance of giving ourselves the necessary space, silence, and stillness for self-awareness. To avoid this, try to understand where your values originate from.

Write down some of the values or beliefs that shape your life and where these come from. Next, decide if these are things that you truly believe in. The first three are done as examples for you.

VALUES	ORIGINS	TRUE FOR ME?
Kindness	Parents	Yes
Appearance	Media	Not in the same way
Wealth	Parents	No

Make it a point to sit down and be introspective more often. When we fill up our lives and leave ourselves with no room to reflect, those distractions (which you analyzed in exercise 1) become our values by default.

Practice this exercise **twice a month** and check if you can note a new value and increase self-awareness. Observing and evaluating are the fundamentals of thinking like a monk. You need to start becoming comfortable with space and stillness.

NOTES

EXERCISE 3A: SELF-REFLECTION

When we are preoccupied, it is very difficult to explore our minds. Sitting at home and doing nothing is not helpful either. There are 3 strategies we suggest for **creating space for self-reflection**.

First, we recommend you sit down and reflect on what happened to you during the day and what you have been feeling emotionally. Write these reflections below to get the hang of it and follow this practice **every day**. Keeping a journal would also be very beneficial.

Day 1

Day 2

Day 3

Day 4

Day 5

Day 6

Day 7

EXERCISE 3B: SELF-REFLECTION

Second, **once a month**, you can jot down new things you have experienced. It may be that you have visited a new place, met someone, left your previous job, or any other change that has occurred (big or small). **Write them down here:**

Month 1

Month 2

Month 3

Month 4

Month 5

EXERCISE 3C: SELF-REFLECTION

Finally, get involved in something meaningful **once a year** - a hobby, a social or political cause, or charity. Write what significant change you have made in your life and how it has impacted you.

Year 1:

Year 2:

NOTES

EXERCISE 4: AUDIT YOUR LIFE REGULARLY

Your actions will always reveal the real story, no matter what you think your life values are. What you do in your spare time shows what you value. For instance, you may consider spending time with your loved ones as your top priority; but if you spend all your free time watching movies or TV shows, your actions don't match your values and you need to do some self-examination.

Spend a week tracking how much time you devote to the following:

Family:

Day 1:

Day 2:

Day 3:

Day 4:

Day 5:

Day 6:

Day 7:

Friends:

Day 1:

Day 2:

Day 3:

Day 4:

Day 5:

Day 6:

Day 7:

Self:

Day 1:

Day 2:

Day 3:

Day 4:

Day 5:

Day 6:

Day 7:

The areas where you spend the most time should ideally match what you value most. If not, that's a sign that you need to re-evaluate your decisions or your values. Note that the focus here is on what you do in your "free time."

Audit your life **once a month** and check if you are getting any closer to your goals. If yes, maintain your habits. If not, review your actions and make changes in your approach.

NOTES

EXERCISE 5: EVALUATE YOUR EXPENSES

In this exercise, you have to make a list of your spending in the past month, excluding necessities like rent, groceries, bills, and loan payments.

Check if your spending corresponds with what matters most to you.

When you look at your monthly expenses, do your purchases result from long or short-term thinking? Are they primarily for entertainment or self-improvement? Decide if each expense is worth it and has any long-term reward.

SPENDING:

1.

2.

3.

4.

5.

6.

7.

8.

9.

10.

11.

Evaluate your expenses **once a month** and check if you have cut down on unnecessary spending. If yes, maintain your habits. If not, review and make changes in your approach, cut down on unnecessary expenses and material needs and **become a conscious buyer!**

NOTES

EXERCISE 6: PAST CHOICES AND THEIR SIGNIFICANCE

At one point in time, we all have to make a choice, either we like it or not.

This exercise helps you to learn from past experiences, both good and bad. Try to repeat the good and avoid the bad.

Note down the three best and three worst choices you have made so far in your life:

Best:

1.

2.

3.

Worst:

1.

2.

3.

QUESTIONS FOR EACH:

1. Why did you make this choice?
2. What have you learned from it?
3. What would you have done differently?

Write here:

Continue here:

NOTES

EXERCISE 7: NEGATIVE PEOPLE

Negativity is highly contagious; you should try to avoid it at all times. Negativity may come in various forms.

Here is a list of "types of negative people." Consider whether you have any of the following types of people in your life.

Write them down:

- **The complainers** (people who are always having "the worst day" but never listen to you):

- **The cancellers** (people who postpone calls, meetings, and hangouts for no real reason):

- **The casualties** (people who think everyone is always against them):

- **The critics** (people who do not support your ambitions or dreams):

- **The commanders** (people who demand you give them attention 24/7):

- **The competitors** (people who compare themselves to you):

- **The controllers** (people who try to manage you):

The aim here is **not** to continually judge negative behaviors but instead, try to neutralize or respond to them with positivity. For example, if a controller says, "we can go out only before my workout and after my lunch meeting", you can say: "Let's find a time that works best for both of us." Practice neutralizing and changing negativity with positivity.

NOTES

EXERCISE 8: COMPANIONS

Make a list of the people with whom you spend the majority of your time over the course of a week. List the values that you **share** and how much time you spend with each person.

NAMES　　　　　　　　**TIME**　　　　　　　　**VALUES**

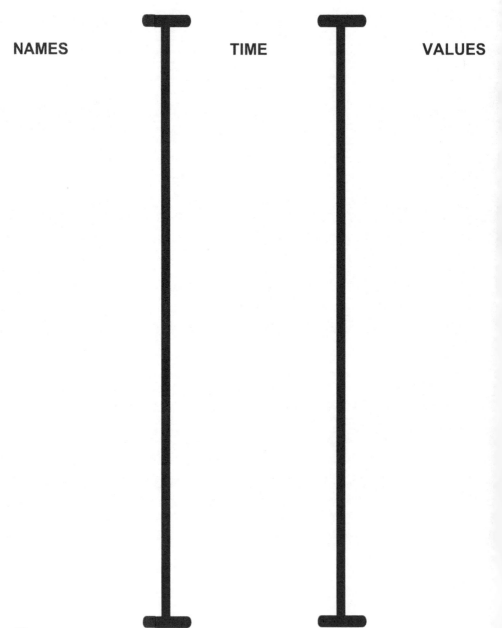

Do the values of people you spend most of your time with align with your values? If not, spend more time with people who share the same values.

Once a month, check if you have started to spend more time with people whose values are similar to yours. If not, make changes in your approach. This way, you will distance yourself from negativity.

NOTES

EXERCISE 9: SELF-AWARENESS

Monks practice **self-awareness** to purify their thoughts and actions.

This is a very important exercise that will help you gain control over your thinking and feelings, as well as automatic reactions. First, try and become aware of a feeling or issue - **spot it**. Then pause for a while to address what the feeling is and where it is coming from - **stop** to consider it. At last, amend your behavior - **swap** in a new way of processing the feeling.

By the end of this exercise, you should be aware of the feelings or problems you are facing and how they can be resolved. It could take you a couple of months to achieve this goal, so be patient.

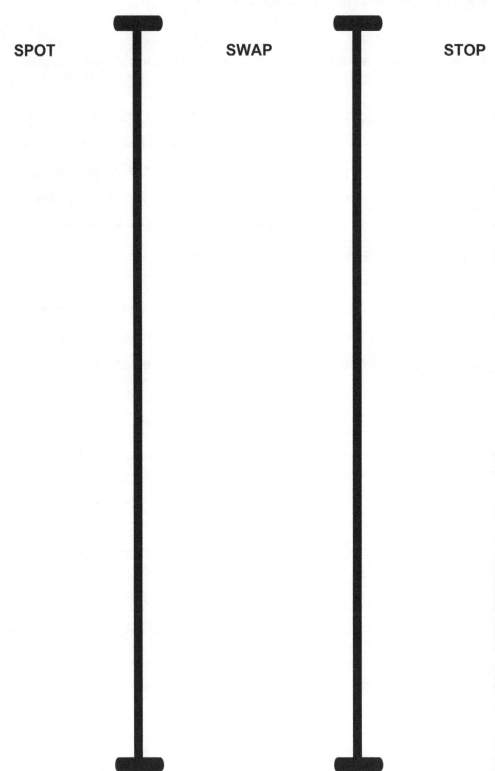

SPOT

SWAP

STOP

NOTES

EXERCISE 10: NEGATIVE COMMENTS

Say no to negative comments! Keep a count of the negative remarks you make over the course of 1 week. Consciously put in the effort to decrease the number of these negative remarks:

Day 1:

Day 2:

Day 3:

Day 4:

Day 5:

Day 6:

Day 7:

Don't stop at day 7 if you haven't reached the goal which is **nil negative comments**. Eliminate these negative comments completely.

NOTES

EXERCISE 11A: REVERSE ENVY

Unfortunately, toxicity is all around us. Unless you clean your heart and inspire others around you to do the same, there will always be mental and emotional pollution around you. These exercises focus on eradicating pollution by cleansing your own heart and thoughts.

Fill in the list of 5 people below that you really care about, but who at the same time, you feel extremely competitive with. Try to come up with at least one reason why you are envious of each one of them. It could be something that they have achieved, something they are better at, something that is going on well for them, etc.

NAME   **REASON**

EXERCISE 11B: REVERSE ENVY

Now ask yourself:

1. Did that achievement (reason) actually take anything away from you?

2. How did it benefit your friend? Visualize everything good that has come to them from this achievement.

3. Would you like to take any of these things away from your friend if you could, even though you know they won't come to you?

If you are envious, **the envy is robbing you of joy**. Remember that envy is more destructive to you than whatever you are actually envious of. Clean your heart and inspire others around you to do the same.

NOTES

EXERCISE 12: FORGIVE YOURSELF

We have to forgive the mistakes we made in the past, to live a happy life, both in the present and future.

Bring out the observer in you, to understand yourself better and let go of the pain.

Write down all the mistakes you want to forgive yourself. Then, read it out loud or record and play it for yourself whenever you want to reaffirm this forgiveness.

I forgive myself for:

1.

2.

3.

4.

5.

6.

7.

8.

Perform this exercise **twice a year**. Accept your own imperfections and mistakes. Forgive yourself and open the doors to emotional healing.

NOTES

EXERCISE 13: RATE YOUR FEAR TO OVERCOME IT

Think of the worst thing you can imagine happening to you, or something you are terrified of. An instance is a major accident or losing a loved one. Make that event a ten on the line.

Just by doing this simple exercise, you will get some perspective on how small or big your fear really is at the moment. When you fear anything, simply rate it, and understand where it falls, when compared to something that's truly scary.

0   10

NOTES

EXERCISE 14: ATTACHMENTS

Ask yourself: "What am I afraid of losing?"

Start with external things: Is it your house, possessions, wealth, or looks?

Then think about internal things: Is it your success, status, friends, sense of belonging, or reputation? Write them down as well.

Complete the list below with what you are afraid of losing:

EXTERNAL   INTERNAL

EXTERNAL   **INTERNAL**

Both lists are probably the biggest sources of pain in your life - you'd be afraid to take those things away from you.

The task here is to eventually start changing your mental relationships with those things so that you are less attached to them.

Reminder! You can still love your partner, children, house, or money. You can do this without being attached in an unhealthy way. It begins with a simple understanding and acceptance that all things are temporary and that you can't truly own or control anything. If you fully appreciate these things, they can enhance your life rather than be a source of constant fear.

NOTES

EXERCISE 15: THINGS TO DO WHEN YOU PANIC

Use your breath to realign your body and mind. Use your breath to constantly calm yourself and relax.

1. Slowly inhale (4 counts)
2. Hold (4 counts)
3. Exhale (4 counts)
4. Repeat 3-5 times till your heart rate slows down
5. Write down what you experience

Experience 1:

Experience 2:

Experience 3:

Experience 4:

Experience 5

Use this exercise to navigate and manage your breath so that you can let go of panic and stress. This will help you remain calm at all times.

NOTES

EXERCISE 16: FUNDAMENTAL MOTIVATIONS

According to the Hindu philosopher, Bhaktivinoda Thakura, four fundamental motivators drive everything we do. Write down if and how any of these four things have motivated you.

1. **Fear** (being driven by bad health, poverty, death):

2. **Desire** (seeking personal achievement through success at work, wealth and pleasure):

3. **Duty** (motivated by responsibilities, family, and the desire to do things right):

4. **Love** (compelled by care and affection for others and the need to help them):

The longer we hold on to fears, the more they ferment. Eventually, they become toxic. We need to be aware of our fears and let go of them. Fear and desire are short-term motivators; whereas, duty and love are more effective long-term. **Be motivated by the right things.**

NOTES

EXERCISE 17: DESIRES

Write down a strong desire that you have:

Now, ask yourself why you desire it. Some answers could be looking and feeling good, having security, achieving personal growth, etc. The task is to keep questioning yourself until you get to know what the root cause is. Don't negate the causes or intentions that aren't "Good".

Write answers here:

1.

2.

3.

4.

5.

6.

7.

Be aware and understand that if your reasons are not associated with **love, growth, or knowledge**, then the desire may fulfill a practical need but won't be emotionally meaningful. You can be highly satisfied when you are in a state of progress, learning or achievement.

NOTES

PART 2: GROWTH

By the end of Part 1, you should have a better understanding of yourself and learn how to let go. Now that you have tried to understand and eliminate your internal and external obstacles, fears, and negativity, it will be easier for you to grow.

The second stage is **growth**. It focuses on reshaping and constructing your life so that you can make better decisions with clear intentions, purpose, routine, and confidence.

EXERCISE 1A: PASSION & PURPOSE

In this exercise, the aim is to compare your passion, skills, and purpose in life to what you are actually doing.

To understand your passion and purpose, use the quadrant below. It gives you a clear picture and understanding of what you are good at and what you love.

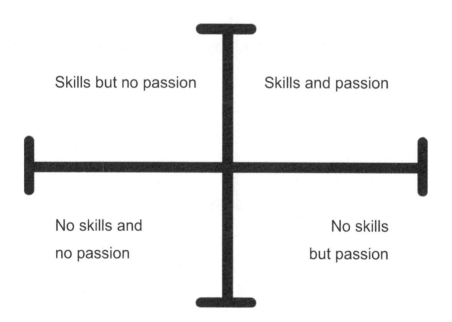

Skills but no passion

Skills and passion

No skills and
no passion

No skills
but passion

Now acknowledge how close you are to living with skills and passion. Fill in the four squares below with things that relate to your job, family, hobbies, and other relationships/friendships.

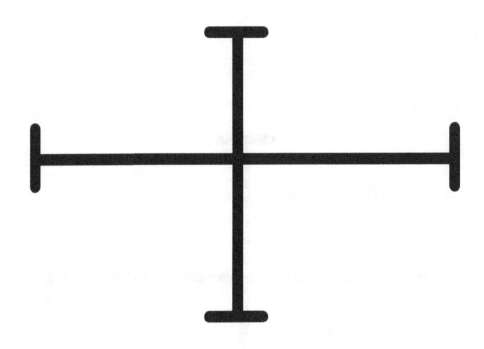

Ideally, whatever fits in the right box is what you should be doing from day to day.

EXERCISE 1B: PASSION & PURPOSE

Finally, write down more things that you are passionate about and compare them with your existing day to day activities:

1.

2.

3.

4.

5.

6.

7.

If you aren't following your purpose, change what you are doing!

NOTES

EXERCISE 2: TURNING YOUR BEST SKILLS INTO ACTIONS

For this exercise, choose a group of people who are close to you and know you well. Consider including people from your workplace, friends, and family members. Use a large number of people between 10 and 20. You can perform this exercise with a smaller group (minimum 3) as well.

Ask your chosen ones to tell you of a time when they think you are at your best. Jot down the most common answers. **Look out for patterns and themes:**

1.

2.

3.

4.

5.

6.

7.

8.

Think about how you can turn your best skills into actions. How can you implement these skills over the weekend? How can you improve your interactions with different people and in different circumstances?

NOTES

EXERCISE 3A: ACTIVITY CHECK AND AWARENESS

You are performing this activity to consciously become more aware of your growth.

At **every month**, note down the activities you have engaged yourself in. These activities may include going out for dinner, running, mediation, preparing a meal, writing emails, meeting friends, speaking to them, spending time on social media, etc. For each activity you perform, ask yourself the two questions that are fundamental to Dharma - Did I enjoy the process? Did others enjoy?

There is no right or wrong answer in this exercise. It simply allows you to make observations to amplify your awareness.

Month 1:

ACTIVITY   DID I ENJOY?   DID OTHERS?

EXERCISE 3B: ACTIVITY CHECK AND AWARENESS

Month 2:

ACTIVITY   DID I ENJOY?   DID OTHERS?

NOTES

EXERCISE 4A: RISING EARLY

Waking up early does not only lead to a more productive day, but also gives you time to do things with purpose. If you wake up "just before" going to work or "just before" going to the gym, then you don't have the time to enjoy your shower, brush teeth properly, eat your breakfast consciously, and make your bed neatly. When you have "just enough time", you actually don't.

The task for this week is for you to wake up fifteen minutes earlier than usual. You may require an alarm; ensure it is a gentle one.

Here is a list of things you are supposed to do after waking up:

- Use dim or natural lighting as soon as you wake up and play quiet or soft music.
- During these fifteen minutes, DO NOT pick up your phone or any other electronics.
- This time is used for giving your brain the space to set the tone for the rest of the day.

Make sure that 30 minutes before you go to sleep, you will have no screen time (TV, phone, laptop, etc.)!

Note down your experience after one week:

WEEK 1:

EXERCISE 4B: RISING EARLY

After week 1, add another fifteen minutes and wake up thirty minutes earlier. Now you have half an hour to yourself.

How will you decide to spend these thirty minutes? For instance, you may want to take a longer shower, extend your meditation or workout time, or enjoy drinking your tea.

Make a list below:

1.

2.

3.

4.

5.

6.

7.

Growth is seen and felt when you are conscious of your every action!

NOTES

EXERCISE 5: T.I.M.E

This is a new way of making your mornings more meaningful.

In the mornings, make time for:

- **Thankfulness**: Express gratitude for the people in your life, your health, wealth, and job. Do this by thinking about it, writing about it, and speaking about it.

- **Insight**: Expand your horizon by reading books and newspapers and listening to podcasts.

- **Meditation**: Spend 15 minutes of your morning meditating and working on your breathing.

- **Exercise**: Keep yourself mentally and physically fit by exercising, stretching, or working out in the morning.

Thankfulness. Insight. Mediation. Exercise. **T.I.M.E.**

Make a morning routine for yourself below:

1. **Thankfulness:**

2. **Insight:**

3. **Meditation**:

4. **Exercise**:

Practice this **every day**. It's even better if you can find a partner to do this exercise with you so you don't miss a single day!

NOTES

EXERCISE 6: POWER OF VISUALIZATION

Visualization is a very powerful tool. Always visualize an idea before building it, just like an inventor. You can have the life you want to live by using the power of visualization. Start by visualizing your mornings.

Write your ideas here and be very detailed:

Read what you write every night and every morning after waking up. Keep reminding yourself of how you want to live your life. **Believe it! Feel it! Live it!**

There could be times when life messes with your plans and things don't go as you have visualized it. Remember that visualization does not change your life; it changes how you see it. Whenever you feel like your life is going off track, you can bring it back with the power of thoughtful visualization.

NOTES

EXERCISE 7: SINGLE AND MULTI-TASKING

Are you a single tasker or a multi tasker? How do you know what you actually are? In most cases, we find ourselves in situations where we have multi tasks or a single task to accomplish. Hence, we don't really know what potential and strength we have.

This exercise is divided into 2 weeks. In the first week, try to do one thing at a time. Do not rush into anything. Try to be at peace and don't juggle. Write down how you feel and what you observe when doing one task at a time.

WEEK 1:

The next week, try to do 2-3 things simultaneously. Juggle between work and keep yourself occupied with personal and work-related things. Now, write down your thoughts for this week. What are your observations on doing multi-tasking?

WEEK 2:

By the end of these exercises, ask yourself which week is more productive, peaceful, and efficient.

Write here which and why:

NOTES

EXERCISE 8: RATE YOUR CONCERN/WORRIES

Things are usually not as bad as you imagine at that particular moment. Give your challenges time and learn from them.

On the perspective scale, rate the following concerns between zero and ten:

a. Losing your job
b. Losing a leg in an accident
c. Waking up late and missing a day at work/school
d. Losing your pet
e. Missing an opportunity
f. Losing your most prized possession
g. Breaking your phone or laptop
h. Losing a loved one

0   10

NOTES

EXERCISE 9: TRANSFORM YOUR EGO

This is an important exercise to grow. Try to look for opportunities that allow you to detach from your ego and **replace it with thoughtful and productive responses.**

Follow these tips in your day-to-day life and note down if you see any changes:

- **Receiving an insult:** Learn to respond to the situation without ego. Take a broader view and observe how your ego reacts to a person's negativity and insults.

- **Receiving negative feedback:** Take a moment to thank the teacher who gives you feedback. Use constructive criticism to your benefit.

- **Arguing with your partner:** Your desire to be right and win an argument comes from your ego's unwillingness to lose and admit weakness. Consider understanding the other person's side as well. Lose the battle and see how it feels.

- **Competing with people:** When people are talking about themselves, you don't always have to add something about yourself to the conversation. Just listen to them. Let them feel good.

NOTES

EXERCISE 10: EGO VS SELF-ESTEEM

If you want to grow, you need to know the difference between positive and negative mindsets. Only then can you begin to change.

In your own words, write down the difference or differences between an inflated ego and a healthy sense of self-esteem:

EGO   **SELF-ESTEEM**

The ego wants to prove itself and self-esteem wants to express itself. Let go of your ego and build your self-esteem.

NOTES

120

EXERCISE 11: CONFIDENCE

Confidence cannot be gained in one day or with one action. It comes from repetition. You need to aim at making small changes and consistently achieve them. This will help increase your confidence.

Pick one from the following areas in which you want to become confident and stable: **health, career, relationships.**

Write down what is going to make you **feel confident** in that particular area. It should be practical, realistic, and achievable.

Write here:

Now, break your chosen area down into small wins and the things that you can achieve TODAY!

Write here:

NOTES

EXERCISE 12A: PRODUCTIVE FEEDBACKS

Select an area in your life that you wish to improve. It could be financial, mental, emotional, or physical.

I want to improve in:

Next, find a person who is an expert in that field and is willing to guide you. Ask him or her relevant questions and if he or she gives you criticism, use it constructively. You can only grow when you accept criticism and work towards building yourself. Spend a **month or two** working on this goal.

Write down what improvements you have made in your chosen area:

NOTES

PART 3: GIVE

By the end of Part 2, you should be able to understand yourself and your growth process better.

Now that we have looked inward, we are ready to look outward at how we interact with others in the world.

The final and most important part of adopting the monk mindset is learning to **give**; looking at the world beyond ourselves and our needs. This involves expanding and sharing our sense of gratitude and deepening our relationships with others. When we share our success and love with others, we discover the true joy and astonishing benefits of service.

EXERCISE 1A: GRATITUDE JOURNAL

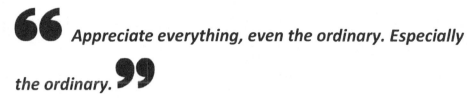 *Appreciate everything, even the ordinary. Especially the ordinary.*

- Pema Chadron

Goal: To appreciate things around you.

First, think about your sleeping habits. What are some issues you have when it comes to sleeping at night?

Write them down:

EXERCISE 1B: GRATITUDE JOURNAL

For a week, write in a gratitude journal every night and track your sleeping habits. Spend five minutes writing down things you are grateful for and see how your sleeping cycle changes. In the morning, write down how many hours you sleep.

Night 1: What are you grateful for? How many hours did you sleep?

Night 2: What are you grateful for? How many hours did you sleep?

Night 3: What are you grateful for? How many hours did you sleep?

Night 4: What are you grateful for? How many hours did you sleep?

Night 5: What are you grateful for? How many hours did you sleep?

Night 6: What are you grateful for? How many hours did you sleep?

Night 7: What are you grateful for? How many hours did you sleep?

Do you see any improvement in your sleep?

NOTES

EXERCISE 2: MORNING GRATITUDE PRACTICE

Gratitude is good for you! Scientifically, thankfulness could have measurable benefits. Gratitude is linked to better mental health, self-awareness, better relationships, and a sense of fulfillment.

Every morning when you wake up, **don't let** your phone be the first thing you look out for. By checking the phone in the morning, it impacts the way your brain is moving and doesn't start your day on a right note.

Try this instead: Take a moment in your bed and flip over on your belly, join your hands and bow your head. Take this moment to show gratitude towards everything you have in your life; a house to live in, clean water to drink, supportive family and friends and the coffee that awaits you.

Practice this for a week and **write down your feelings below:**

Continue here:

NOTES

EXERCISE 3: MEAL GRATITUDE PRACTICE

821 million people in the world go to bed on an empty stomach. That is 1 out of 9 people. When the world is suffering from hunger and malnourishment, take a moment to show gratitude for your meals.

Choose one meal from your day and make it a point to show gratitude for the preparation of the meal. Before you dig in, show gratitude for your food.

Making gratitude a part of your daily routine is the easy part, but your ultimate aim should be to remain grateful at all times and in all circumstances. Even if your life isn't perfect, build your gratitude like a muscle. If you train it every day, it will strengthen over time.

NOTES

EXERCISE 4: GRATITUDE MEDITATION

Practicing meditation for 10-30 minutes a day can help you reduce stress, anxiety, and anger. It can help you sleep better, think better, and live with a more positive and happier outlook on life.

To practice gratitude meditation, you need to start with joy or happiness visualization. During meditation, imagine yourself in a moment when you experienced joy. Allow that feeling of joy to wash over you, carry the feeling throughout the meditation, and try to stretch it over the entire day.

In the last chapters you will find guidelines for meditation.

NOTES

EXERCISE 5: GRATITUDE THROUGH VOLUNTEERING AND SERVICE

Service broadens perspective and eliminates negativity. It also provides a sense of happiness and fulfillment. **Once a month or once a week, volunteer** - give back to the community.

Monks try to practice gratitude throughout the day through small interactions. Incorporate small acts of kindness into your day-to-day life and show gratitude and kindness towards not just loved ones but also strangers.

Reminder! Service is the direct path to a meaningful life.

NOTES

EXERCISE 6A: WRITING A GRATITUDE LETTER OR POSTCARD

Express your gratitude to people in your life. Think of specific moments that you have shared with them. Think ahead what you're going to do or say whenever you meet them again.

Pick 3 people in your life that you feel deeply grateful to:

1.

2.

3.

EXERCISE 6B: WRITING A GRATITUDE LETTER

Write them a gratitude letter or a postcard mentioning the things you love about them and how they have helped you grow into a better person.

Write down how you feel after writing the letter and how the 3 people react to it:

NOTES

EXERCISE 7: GRATITUDE IN HINDSIGHT

Most of us have experienced moments where we were not grateful for something when it happened. Today, think of one such moment where you aren't grateful for something. It could be a breakup or losing a job or ending a friendship or not getting into your top college.

Write experience:

Now, take a moment to consider in what way this experience is worthy of gratitude.

Answer these questions:

1.   Unexpectedly, did you benefit from it?

2.   If yes, how did you benefit from it?

3.   What good has come out right now, from what you had experienced that time?

If something is happening against your will or something you have not anticipated, gain the understanding that there are better opportunities coming your way. **Be grateful for your tough times; they make you into a warrior!**

NOTES

EXERCISE 8: MENTOR AND APPRENTICE

Make a list of your mentors and apprentices (students):

Now write down what the students could teach you and what the mentors could learn from you.

Mentors:

Students:

NOTES

EXERCISE 9: EXTEND YOUR RADIUS OF CARE

Write down the names of 3-4 people for whom you would drop everything:

1.

2.

3.

4.

Think about how many times you tell each one of them that you care about them. Do you ever actually have the time or chance to show that you care for them? What are you going to do?

NOTES

EXERCISE 10: SIX LOVING EXCHANGES

The Upadesamrta speaks about 6 ways of exchanging love between partners in a relationship. Each involves giving and receiving to encourage bonding and growing together.

Gifts

- Giving with intention
- Receiving with gratitude

Conversations

- Listening without judgment
- Speaking with vulnerability

Food

- Preparing without agenda
- Receiving with presence

Try doing these things with your partner and write down how you feel after doing them:

Reminder! These six exchanges can be thoughtless and empty, or they can be deep and meaningful, but don't judge your partner for the efforts he or she has put in.

NOTES

MEDITATION: BREATHWORK, VISUALIZATION, CHANTING

There is no better tool to help you find flexibility and control than meditation. Through meditation, we find clarity and we can be who we really want to be in a given moment. Our breath connects to our mind, and our mind can visualize what we want. You can enhance this process by chanting. What you visualize and chant is what you receive.

Breathe to calm yourself and relax. Once you have gained control of your breathing, start visualizing. Keep it simple and don't force yourself.

Here are tips for everyday meditation, visualization, and powerful breathing patterns that increase focus and stillness.

PREPARATION: WARM-UP

Before starting your meditation follow the steps below:

1. Find a comfortable spot - a chair, the floor, a cushion. Avoid meditating on your bed.
2. Make yourself comfortable.
3. Keep your back straight and upright.
4. Make yourself aware of your surroundings.
5. Try to avoid distractions and close your eyes slowly and gently.
6. Inhale and exhale slowly.
7. Bring your awareness to:
   - Calm
   - Balance
   - Ease
   - Stillness
   - Peace

   It's perfectly alright if your mind wanders sometimes, just gently bring it back to those five things.

   - Calm
   - Balance
   - Ease
   - Stillness
   - Peace

8. Now become aware of your breathing pattern. Count the number of breaths. Don't force your breath, just become aware of it.

9. Feel your breath - no rush, no pressure. Start simple, soft, gentle breathing at your own pace, at your own time.

Breathe to calm and relax yourself.

Once you have gained control of your breathing, start visualizing. Keep it simple. Don't force yourself.

TODAY AND FOREVER

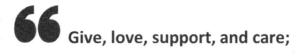 Give, love, support, and care;

today and forever!

The monk mentality is about living in the present but also about today and forever. As you know, life is not measured by the days we live but by the impact we create and how people make us feel.

To think like a monk, be grateful for everything, act consciously and follow your purpose every single day.

CONGRATULATIONS ON FINISHING THIS WORKBOOK!

We hope that you have found this workbook **valuable** and had an **enjoyable experience**.

We always **strive to improve** ourselves to **deliver the highest quality of work** to you.

But **we cannot improve without you**. If you like our efforts, **please support us** by giving us a quick review of the workbook on its Amazon page. Your support will allow us to produce products of even **better quality** in the future.

Thank you!

The Intensive Life Publishing Team

ABOUT INTENSIVE LIFE PUBLISHING

We live in a fast-paced world; everyone is always doing something. We started *Intensive Life Publishing* so that we can help people ***get key ideas fast***. Our mission is to provide you with **accurate, well-written workbooks and summaries** of some of the world's best-selling books so that you, as our reader, can **get the valuable information that you need**. This also, in turn, promotes those fantastic, best-selling books and their respective authors.

To know more about Intensive Life Publishing, you can visit **intensivelife.com** and **follow us** on social media:

 @intensivelifepublishing

 @intensive_life

Made in the USA
Las Vegas, NV
29 April 2024